COPYRIGHT © KASHAN AJMERI 2024

All rights reserved. No part of this book may be reproduced, stored, or transmitted in any form or by any means, electronic, mechanical, photocopying, recording, scanning, or otherwise, without the prior written permission of the publisher, except for brief quotations embodied in critical reviews and certain other noncommercial uses permitted by copyright law.

For permissions requests or inquiries, contact:

Whatsapp +1 6234049756

Published by Kashan Ajmeri

BREAKING BARRIERS THE REAL STORY OF MY REMARKABLE JOURNEY

Welcome to "Breaking Barriers: The Real Story of My Remarkable Journey."

In the pages of this book, you'll embark on a deeply personal expedition through the twists and turns of my life's journey. It's a narrative that resonates with the raw emotions of triumph, defeat, resilience, and ultimately, hope.

Growing up, I never imagined the hurdles life would throw my way. But as I faced each obstacle head-on, I discovered a strength within me that I never knew existed. From humble beginnings marked by adversity to the heights of success attained through sheer determination, my journey is a testament to the power of the human spirit.

Along the way, I've weathered storms, navigated uncharted territories, and emerged stronger and wiser. This book is not just a recollection of events; it's a testament to the resilience of the human soul. It's about breaking free from the constraints of circumstance, defying expectations, and embracing the endless possibilities that life has to offer.

Through candid reflections, heartfelt anecdotes, and moments of vulnerability, I invite you to walk alongside me as I unravel the layers of my life story. From the lowest lows to the highest highs, each chapter is a testament to the indomitable human spirit and the unwavering belief that anything is possible with determination and perseverance.

So, dear reader, join me on this remarkable journey—a journey of self-discovery, growth, and transformation. Let us embark together on a quest to break barriers, defy the odds, and embrace the extraordinary potential that lies within each of us. Together, let's discover the true meaning of resilience and the boundless power of the human spirit. Welcome to "Breaking Barriers: The Real Story of My Remarkable Journey."

Yes, this is my real story. I've experienced many ups and downs in my life, and I've hidden my pain and struggles. I've lost myself in trying to please others, but eventually, I set goals and gave my life a purpose. After reading this book, I hope my readers will never give up in their lives. They will believe in themselves during tough times and work hard to achieve their goals. Life brings challenges, but never give up.

Hello everyone, my name is Kashan Ajmeri. I hail from Karachi, Pakistan, and I'm currently 28 years old. I was born on March 23, 1996, in Karachi. I come from a middle-class family. I am a Muslim. I obtained my education from a secondary school, but I wasn't much of a studious student. My main goal was to pass my matriculation exams and apply for a government job, as it is the dream of around 90% of the young generation in Pakistan.

After passing my matric exams, I started going to the gym to maintain my fitness, as I wanted to apply for the army. In my family, there were my father, mother, an elder brother, myself, a sister, and a younger brother; a small but close-knit family. I found some good friends in school, especially my late best friend Shahjahan, who tragically passed away in a drowning accident at the beach in 2017.

I had a few other friends like Asad Magsi and Waqar, but my interest was not in academics. After passing my 10th grade, I applied to join the Pakistan Army, but unfortunately, I was rejected because I fell short of the required height of 5.6 inches, standing at 5.4 inches. I was devastated and felt dejected when I came back home and shared the news with my family.

My father, seeing my disappointment, motivated me, saying it's not the end and there's still plenty of time. He encouraged me to start stretching exercises, which could potentially help me meet the height requirement.

So, I started my stretching routine and began going to the park for morning runs. After a couple of months, I decided to apply for a position in the Pakistan Coast Guard. I went to their headquarters early in the morning and, despite the rush, managed to meet with a Major and submit my documents. They gave me a receipt and scheduled a date for my running and physical tests.

Excitedly, I shared the news with my family and prepared diligently for the tests. This was in 2016 when I was applying for a government job for the second time. My father had retired from BOC Gas Company, and my elder brother had been studying. With my father's retirement payout, my family decided to invest in a small school to provide free education for underprivileged children.

Despite being from a middle-class family, I was aware of the importance my parents placed on education. When the day of my physical test arrived, I was confident due to my daily training routine. I completed the running test and was instructed to return after an hour for further tests.

My family was overjoyed when I returned home to share the news of my success. After a quick break, I headed back to headquarters for the next phase of my physical assessment.

So, I arrived for my further tests and managed to qualify. I was very happy, feeling like this job was finally going to be mine. I had applied for the position of Sepoy General Duty. After my physical tests, I was taken for medical examinations, which took around 15 to 16 hours. I didn't eat dinner or lunch, feeling extremely tired after the tests. When I returned home around 10 p.m., having gone there at 8 a.m. the previous morning, I informed my family that I had passed all the tests.

DEAR READER,

Thank you for taking the time to read

"Breaking Barriers The Real Story of My Remarkable Journey "

Your feedback is incredibly valuable to me as an author. If you enjoyed the book and found it helpful in any way, I would be truly grateful if you could leave an honest review on Amazon or any other platform where you purchased or read the book.

Your review not only helps other readers discover the book but also provides me with valuable insights into what resonated with you and how I can continue to improve as a writer.

Thank you once again for your support and for being a part of this journey with me.

With gratitude,
Author
Kashan Ajmeri

However, despite all my efforts and stretching, I was rejected due to my height, as I had only managed to increase it by one inch. But I didn't let myself feel demotivated in front of my family. I assured them that it was okay and that I would apply again for the next vacancies. I continued with my fitness routine and stretching.

However, sometime later, I was out with friends while my sister and younger brother were at school, and my mother and elder brother were at the school we had bought. Only my father was at home. When I returned from the outing, I noticed a lot of neighbors gathered near my house and some were even inside.

I immediately felt something was wrong. I rushed closer to my house and found out that my father's health had deteriorated significantly. A local doctor from our area informed me that his condition was serious and advised taking him to the hospital immediately. I was terrified. I quickly called my elder brother and arranged for a taxi to take us to the government hospital since I didn't have enough money. At the hospital, we learned that my father had suffered a stroke.

I was devastated. My elder brother and other family members arrived at the hospital, and we spent the next 24 hours there. Eventually, we decided to transfer him to a private hospital for better treatment, using some savings we had from my father's retirement and the school we owned.

At the private hospital, my father was kept for 3 to 4 days. After that, we were informed that his condition had become critical, and he needed to be put on a ventilator. My family was at home, but my elder brother had been at the hospital for the past 4 days and didn't want to leave our father alone.

He insisted that the doctors shift our father to the ventilator. He was very upset. In the evening, my mother and relatives went to the hospital and were told about our father's critical condition and the need for a ventilator. We were all terrified because we had never experienced such a situation before. I loved my father very much, and I couldn't bear to see him like that. I spent the entire night in the hospital garden, crying and praying.

The next day, when it was time to visit patients at 7 p.m., I saw my father with his eyes closed and a ventilator tube in his mouth. I was in a lot of pain and fear. That night, the doctors handed my brother the bill and informed him that our father had passed away. My brother remained composed, but I could see the sadness in his eyes. I went downstairs to the reception area, where I saw my elder brother, my uncle, my mother's brothers, and my father's close friends.

They were all discussing what had happened. When I heard them say that my father had passed away, I started crying. My brother confirmed that it was true. We hugged each other and cried a lot.

Then we went to console our mother, who was devastated. We shared the news with everyone and tried to console each other, but we couldn't stop crying, realizing that our father was no longer with us.

After bringing my father's body home, we informed all our family members and relatives and told them that our father was no longer with us. We buried him in the graveyard, and for a few days, we remained saddened by his loss.

We reminisced about our father and tried to console our mother, hoping to ease her pain. Life continued after our father's death. We used up our savings for his treatment at the private hospital, leaving us with nothing.

My elder brother and I decided to find jobs to support our family and ensure our younger siblings' education. We sold our school to cover our father's medical expenses. Our house was small, and we had no other resources.

Due to my fitness and gym routine, I was offered a job as a security guard, which I accepted for the sake of my family. My elder brother also applied for jobs and eventually found work as an accountant at a salon and spa. However, the security guard job didn't last long for me. At that time, I was only 18 years old, with no beard on my face, and looking very young. I became worried and started searching for another job.

Afterward, I got a job as a salesman at a shopping mall. I attended an interview and passed, starting my new job shortly after. I worked hard, but due to the job, my fitness declined, and I had to give up my gym routine.

I couldn't afford transportation, so I walked 10 to 12 kilometers to work every day. Despite this, our financial situation remained unstable. Time passed, and life continued with its ups and downs. My elder brother's job was going well, but we still weren't financially stable.

Then came a happy moment in our lives when we decided it was time for my elder brother to get married. We found a suitable match for him, and the engagement took place.

However, our small house had only one room, so we decided to rent a larger house instead of renovating our own due to frequent leaks during rainy seasons. We couldn't afford the renovations required for renting it out. After renting a bigger house, my elder brother got married, and our lives returned to normalcy.

Later, I found out about job openings in the police force. I prepared my documents and decided to apply. My elder brother advised me to continue my studies while he managed the household. However, I knew he wasn't financially stable either. He had borrowed money for the wedding and had monthly loan installments to pay.

I decided to work and not continue my education, as it would have put financial strain on my brother. I applied for a job in the police force online, continuing my journey.

After applying for a job in the police force, I was constantly worried and anxious about how I would pass the physical tests. My job at the mall was tough, with working hours from 3 pm to 3 am. I would often feel exhausted by the time I got home and struggled to wake up early for training. However, I thought that walking 10 to 12 kilometers to work every day would be enough to maintain my fitness.

As time passed, the date for the police physical tests approached. When I arrived at the training center at 5 am, I saw many candidates who were also there for the tests, all looking for job opportunities.

Unfortunately, the physical tests took longer than expected, and by the time my running test was scheduled, it was already 1 pm, and I was exhausted and thirsty. Due to my fatigue, I couldn't perform well in the running test and ended up failing.

I was extremely disappointed, especially since my father, who had always motivated me, was no longer with us. I returned home that evening and informed my family about my failure.

The next day, I resumed my job at the mall. Over the next three years, I continued working there while also applying for positions in the armed forces. However, my physical fitness wasn't up to par, and I struggled to meet the requirements. Despite repeatedly applying and attempting the tests, I continued to fail, feeling frustrated and disappointed.

After numerous failed attempts at the physical tests and a lot of time spent applying, I decided it was time to leave my job at the mall and seek office employment. I discussed this decision with my elder brother, who mentioned that his friend's office needed a data specialist.

I agreed to give it a try and applied for the position. I was scheduled for an interview at 4 p.m. I had little experience in office environments and didn't know what to expect.

I usually avoided taking the bus, but circumstances forced me to rely on it this time. Arriving at the office, I was struck by its size and luxury. I informed the receptionist of my interview appointment with Shahrayz Anwer and was asked to wait. I waited for some time as the boss was in his office, separate from his family, who were also present in the office. They were resting, which meant I had to wait a while longer.

After a while, the boss called me into the conference room, where he reviewed my resume (CV) and asked if I knew how to use a laptop, to which I replied in the affirmative.

The interview concluded with a few questions, and he told me to wait for his call. He then mentioned that the job was currently for the night shift and asked if I was willing to work it. I agreed but inquired if the night shift was permanent.

He reassured me that it was temporary. I agreed to take the job and waited for his call. Upon returning home, I resumed my job at the mall. However, a few days later, while returning from my late-night job, I was chased by mobile snatchers. Luckily, there were police patrolling in the area, and the snatchers fled.

I managed to reach home safely. The next day, before heading to work, I received a call from Shahrayz Anwer's office, offering me the job.

That night marked my first shift at a US-based mortgage loan agency, which worked with well-known institutions like Wells Fargo and Bank of America. I was thrilled to have landed a good job and started my work that same night. Interestingly, both the office and the boss shared the same name, Shahrayz Anwer.

I arrived at the office on time at 7:30 p.m. and was briefed by an experienced colleague on my tasks. I quickly understood my duties and began working.

When the boss asked if I understood the tasks, I confidently replied yes, as it was a straightforward job of filtering data from 500 leads. I started working at 10 p.m. and managed to complete the task in just 3 to 4 hours. I sent the filtered leads to the boss via email.

He was impressed and asked how I managed to finish a 12-hour task in such a short time. I couldn't explain it, but he seemed satisfied with the results after checking the leads himself. He praised my work, and my shift ended.

I went home and shared the good news with my elder brother, who was happy for me. He had been like a father figure to me since our father's passing, always caring for me as if I were his son.

Life had improved significantly. My boss, Shahrayz Anwer, was extremely kind and had a friendly nature. He provided lunch, tea, and other amenities for free, and he was always willing to cooperate, even offering advance payments when needed. After working there for a few days, my best friend, Idrees, expressed his need for a job. He was working as a salesman at a Levi's shop but wanted to change jobs. When I told my boss about Idrees' situation, he agreed to interview him for a position, even though there were no vacancies at the time.

I brought Idrees to the office the next morning, and my boss conducted the interview.

He decided to hire Idrees for the night shift, knowing that Idrees had never worked the night shift before, as his parents were worried about his safety. However, I assured them that he would be fine, and they agreed. On Idrees' first day, I helped him understand his tasks, and we were given a room to work together.

We played music while working and were both very happy with our jobs. Our boss was supportive in every way, providing us with biscuits, chocolates, and other treats whenever we wanted. Idrees was thrilled with his new job, as he had found not only employment but also a great boss who cared for us both.

As the days went by, things were looking up. My family had arranged my marriage with my cousin, and my job was going well with a good salary. Six months later, I was getting married, and I was very happy.

I had a good job and a good salary, and now my marriage was on the horizon. However, then came the news of a virus that had spread worldwide, named the coronavirus or COVID-19.

The virus caused businesses to slow down, and many people lost their jobs as lockdowns were implemented. We were also worried about the situation. My boss informed us that his business was also slowing down and that he couldn't afford to keep both Idrees and me employed.

He tried to find a solution to keep us on, but the business downturn was severe. Eventually, he said he couldn't afford to keep us anymore.

We were devastated, but our boss understood our financial situation. He offered to give us three months' salary in advance until we found other jobs. Due to COVID-19, job opportunities were scarce. Idrees and I were both worried and anxious.

My wedding was approaching, but my elder brother had to take a bank loan to cover the expenses, as we also had my sister's wedding to consider. I wanted to support my brother financially for both weddings, but I didn't have enough money.

I felt overwhelmed because my elder brother was already burdened with responsibilities like paying rent, electricity bills, grocery bills, and my younger brother's school fees. I knew I had to find a solution, so I began thinking about acquiring new skills and started researching which skills were in demand.

So I did some research and understood that social media marketing is the best option. I started searching online and joined an institute to learn Social Media Marketing. After learning social media marketing, I was unsure of what to do next because until I practically ran ads, I couldn't offer my services as I had neither clients nor experience.

Then I thought of starting an e-commerce business because I had marketing skills. I knew I could do the marketing for my business and run ads, gaining experience in the process.

But the issue was how to start an e-commerce business as I didn't have enough money, and it was just two months before my wedding. Then I contacted a local supplier who dealt with mobile phones, and I started working as a reseller with him.

I ran my ad and received many messages, but I wasn't good at dealing with customers initially. However, after some time, I received my first order, and I got a good commission from it.

I understood that if I worked properly, I could generate a good amount. So I started working early in the morning and made deals with customers. I saved some money and used it to contribute to my brother's wedding expenses.

My brother was happy when I told him about this opportunity, and soon after, I got married. I worked hard after marriage, and my business flourished. Then, God blessed me with a beautiful daughter named Shehzeen, who was a huge gift for me. Time passed, and my responsibilities increased, especially due to the deteriorating economy because of COVID-19. Everything became expensive, and my brother and I decided to run the household together.

However, the business started slowing down, and sometimes, I received complaints about the quality of imports, which made mobile phones expensive, leading to a decline in sales. Paying rent became a concern, so we decided to sell our own house to buy a bigger one where our family could adjust.

However, we didn't get as much money as we expected from the sale, so we saved the money in the bank and decided to continue saving to buy a better house. I was troubled due to the business, and my brother also had many responsibilities.

I thought nowadays people earn a lot through Amazon, so I took an Amazon VA course, but I couldn't understand it well, wasting both time and money.

Then I thought about what to do next, considering the high expenses at home. Many times, I had to borrow money from friends and my brother, which made me very anxious. I had taken a lot of money from my friends and brother. So I thought, why not start blogging now? At this time, with the help of ChatGPT, writing articles became very easy.

I bought domain hosting and created a blog website named Mahkash.com. I posted many articles and did SEO, but there wasn't much traffic on my website. After that, I applied for Google Adsense, but unfortunately, my website was rejected.

Now my blogging website couldn't help me much, and I was quite worried. The business was slow, and I didn't have a job either. Expenses were increasing, and I couldn't apply for a government job because I was overage for the forces, as they only accept candidates aged 18 to 23.

I spent time in responsibilities and struggles, and the idea of a government job faded away with time as I became overage. Now I had to choose between a job or business. I knew a job would only support my family, while a business would benefit my entire family.

I decided to continue with my business. I worked hard, but Pakistan's economic situation was tough in January 2024, and my business was slow. I then thought of starting work on Amazon Kindle, but I didn't have much knowledge about it.

I watched YouTube videos to learn, and I understood how to sell books on Amazon. I decided to write a book, and my first book's title and topic were related to social media marketing.

I wrote the book and wanted to publish it on Amazon, but its format wasn't correct, and it wasn't approved. After more research, I understood the format and published the book, but it didn't make any sales. Alongside this, I continued working on mobile repairs to clear the household expenses.

After some time, I started writing books again and began publishing one book daily. Alongside this, I continued my mobile sales business. I wrote mystery books, thriller novels, action books, and various other genres. Maybe some would sell. After writing 10 books, I learned about KDP and Kindle Unlimited.

I started promoting my books on Kindle Unlimited, and after promoting some free books, I received an order for a paperback version of my biography of Mukesh Ambani, earning me a $2 commission and seeing that $2 in my dashboard after months of hard work filled me with joy and motivation.

I continued writing and eventually earned $6. However, I felt upset when I noticed that buyers on Kindle Unlimited could buy books for free but didn't read them.

I couldn't understand why they bought them if they weren't going to read them. Nevertheless, I continued writing books and realized the importance of reviews in reaching a wider audience.

I created a review page for each book, but so far, only three books received 2 or 3 ratings, which left me disappointed. Despite this, I remained determined to continue writing books.

I learned that Amazon ads could greatly help sales, but I didn't have enough money to run ads on Amazon Kindle. If I became a successful author, I knew my life would be set, and I could provide a better life for my family and financially support my elder brother.

My wife, friends, and family supported and loved me, and they all wanted me to become a successful author. Today, on April 24, 2024, I decided to write this book and worked hard on it. My journey continues until I become a successful author.

I also made efforts on my YouTube channel, "mk Ajmeri SMC," where I created videos on social media marketing, but due to time constraints, I had to stop. Now, my dream is to succeed on Amazon and see my books sell well. I wake up early in the morning to write books and dedicate time to my mobile-selling business at 10 am.

My dream is to provide a better future for my family and financially support my elder brother.

I am grateful to those who take the time to read my books. Your support and feedback matter a lot to me as an author. Thank you for giving my book your time and consideration.

www.ingramcontent.com/pod-product-compliance
Lightning Source LLC
Chambersburg PA
CBHW081020240526
45471CB00018B/3918